The Story
of
Manchester United

Special thanks to:
Mike Edey

Foreword

Sometimes we can't put into words why we support a football team – we just do.

Often in the school playground the decision is no more scientific than 'I liked the colour of their shirt'.

Whatever the reason, *The Story of Manchester United* is one which will reassure children they have made a fine choice and help parents like myself ensure that their youngsters are brought up on only the best reading material!

For fan or foe, the Manchester United story is one of highs, lows, excitement, adventure and poignancy. It is a story for those who follow the team of no villains – only heroes. Enjoy.

Eamonn Holmes

Manchester United are the biggest football club in the world.

They have been champions of Europe twice and have won the Premiership nine times, more than any other club.

United have the biggest club stadium in Britain and play all their home games in front of more than 76,000 supporters.

But they have not always been a team of millionaire superstars – and they have not always been called Manchester United.

In fact, they have not always played in the famous red shirts; their first kit was green and gold ...

The club was formed in 1878 by a group of football-crazy railway workers. They called themselves Newton Heath L.Y.R. (Lancashire and Yorkshire Railway).

In the beginning they only played against other railway teams because they did not think they were good enough to play against the big teams in the Football League like Blackburn Rovers, Aston Villa and Sheffield United.

Not playing against the big teams meant Newton Heath soon became poor and it was feared they would close forever.

Thankfully, a brewery owner called John Henry Davies came to the rescue.

He only discovered Newton Heath had run out of money when he found club captain Henry Stafford's missing dog and Henry told him all about the problems. The club had been saved by a St Bernard!

John Henry Davies decided to change the name of the club – but didn't like Manchester Central or Manchester Celtic.

So, Manchester United was born in 1902.

James West was named manager, but lasted only three games before Ernest Mangnall took control. Success would soon follow.

Just two seasons later United finished as runners-up in the Second Division and were now in the top flight.

And things were to get even better after they signed Billy Meredith – nicknamed the Welsh Wizard – from Manchester City.

Billy helped United win the League Championship for the first time in 1908 and kept on playing football until he was 51!

Just a year later, Ernest's boys also won the FA Cup for the first time, beating Bristol City 1–0 in the final.

F. & J. SMITH'S CIGARETTES

MANCHESTER UNITED.
W. MEREDITH.

The club was not just moving forward **on** the pitch, they also moved **off** it in 1910 – from their old home at Bank Street to a brand new stadium called Old Trafford.

Just two days later the old wooden stand at Bank Street was blown down by strong winds.

United had moved in the nick of time!

OLD TRAFFORD

Old Trafford was opened on February 19, 1910 and was described as the best football stadium in the world. It cost £60,000 – a fortune at the time – and had a capacity of 80,000.

The stadium was bombed during the Second World War and parts had to be rebuilt. It re-opened in 1949 and looked exactly as it had before the war.

A year later a roof was added to the legendary Stretford End – which packed in 20,000 fanatical United fans.

Floodlights were first installed in the 1950s.

The last game played in front of the Stretford End was a 3–1 win over Tottenham Hotspur in 1992 – then it was replaced by a £10million all-seated stand.

By 1995 the huge three-tiered North Stand had been built to hold 26,000 fans.

The East and West Ends were made bigger too, and in 2006 the capacity was increased to more than 76,000 – making it the biggest club stadium in Britain.

It is hoped the stadium will become even bigger. Extending the South Stand would allow an amazing 96,000 fans to watch United.

United would go on to win the league for the second time the following year, but the good days quickly ended.

Most fans blamed manager Ernest Mangnall when the club finished 13th – so he left and joined Manchester City.

Over the next 15 years more managers arrived at Old Trafford than trophies.

United were now so poor on the pitch that they were relegated and so poor off it they could not pay the players' wages. Rival fans even nicknamed them 'the Rags'.

In 1930, the Reds made the worst start in their history, losing their first 12 league matches and letting in 115 goals in just one season.

The fans were so fed-up that just 3,507 turned up to the opening match of the next season.

Local businessman James Gibson gave United £30,000 to pay the players but they still came within one game of the unthinkable – being relegated to the Third Division (League One today).

In that same week in 1934, City won the FA Cup.
Playing for them that day was a man called Matt Busby …

Matt would later famously cross the city divide but before he did he was captain of United's other great rivals, Liverpool. United played yo-yo football for many years – being relegated then promoted, then relegated then promoted.

The Second World War broke out in 1939 and English football was put on hold for a few years. Old Trafford did not escape the horror – the stadium was bombed during a German air raid in 1941 and the main stand was destroyed.

Matt served in the army during the war where he proved he was a great leader of men. It was here that he met a man called Jimmy Murphy. Matt overheard Jimmy giving a speech to encourage his soldiers one day and was so impressed that he would later offer him a job.

After the war, Liverpool wanted Matt back and offered more money but he joined United as manager in 1945 and would still be at the club 25 years later.

Matt made his old comrade Jimmy Murphy his assistant. It was his first signing and some say his best. With Jimmy by his side, Matt would change United forever. After just three years in charge his boys won the FA Cup – the club's first cup win for 39 years.

United finished second four times between 1945 and 1952 and impatient fans wanted the manager to sign big stars. But the super Scot was determined to give young players their chance.

Jackie Blanchflower, Roger Byrne, Duncan Edwards, Mark Jones, David Pegg, Eddie Colman, Bill Foulkes, Dennis Viollet and Tommy Taylor all came into the side – and won over the fans.

They became known as the Busby Babes.

BUSBY BABES

Most of the Busby Babes played for United's youth side but even though they were very young they were so good Matt Busby decided he could not leave them out of the first team.

And in 1956 United – with an average age of 22 – won the title for the first time in 45 years. They also won it the following year, with Bobby Charlton now in the team.

The star players were Tommy Taylor and Duncan Edwards. Tommy was signed from Barnsley for £29,999 – the extra pound went to the tea lady because Matt did not want Tommy to have to put up with the added pressure of being the first player in the world to cost £30,000.

Tommy went on to become one of United's greatest ever goalscorers – scoring an amazing 131 goals in 191 games.

Duncan was the Wayne Rooney of his day. In April 1953, he became the First Division's youngest-ever player at the age of 16 years and 185 days. He was very strong for his age, was fast and had an amazing shot. Some people who saw him play say he was the greatest player ever.

Tommy and Duncan were two of the eight Busby Babes who died in the 1958 Munich air disaster.

In 1957–58 United were going for three titles in a row. At the start of February they beat Arsenal 5–4 in a thriller at Highbury.

It was the last time the Busby Babes would play on British soil …

Matt's boys had already proved they were the best team in England and were beginning to show they were the best in Europe too.

They knocked out Red Star Belgrade to reach the semi-final of the European Cup (now called the Champions League) but on the way home, disaster struck.

After refuelling at Munich Airport on February 6, 1958, the plane carrying United's brilliant young team crashed.

On that day, 21 people were killed, including seven players – David Pegg, Liam Whelan, Eddie Colman, Roger Byrne, Geoff Bent, Tommy Taylor and Mark Jones.

Duncan Edwards became the eighth player to die 15 days later.

A unique team had been taken away from a unique club.

Matt Busby was badly hurt in the accident but bravely won his battle for life.

After building one of the greatest football teams Britain has ever seen, he had to start all over again.

Bill Foulkes and Bobby Charlton survived the Munich crash and went on to enjoy great careers at Old Trafford.

Nobby Stiles broke through then Busby made two brilliant signings – Denis Law from Torino and a young good-looking lad from Belfast called George Best.

Denis scored the first goal in the 1963 FA Cup win over Leicester City. United were back!

George's unbelievable skills and Denis's incredible scoring record meant the Reds won their sixth championship two years later and were once again back in Europe …

In March 1966 they beat Benfica 1–0 at Old Trafford – then thrashed them 5–1 away, scoring three times in the first 15 minutes. Some say it was George's finest game for the club.

After winning the league the following season, Matt was rewarded with another attempt at the greatest trophy of all – the European Cup.

In the final, at Wembley, they met Benfica again. Bobby Charlton opened the scoring but Jaime Graca equalised with ten minutes left and the game went into extra-time.

Nervous fans could hardly watch but Matt's boys destroyed Benfica with three memorable goals in seven glorious minutes – from George Best, Brian Kidd and Bobby Charlton.

So, just ten years after the horror of Munich, United were champions of Europe – the first English club to win the famous trophy.

SIR MATT BUSBY

Alexander Matthew Busby was born in Bellshill, Scotland on May 26, 1909.

He began his career at Manchester City then signed for Liverpool, where he was made captain, before becoming United manager in 1945.

Matt began to turn the club around and the Reds finished second in the league in 1947, 1948, 1949 and 1951 before finally winning it in 1952.

Matt was seriously injured in the Munich air crash and doctors feared he would die. But he showed his incredible fighting spirit by pulling through, and returned to Old Trafford to rebuild his team.

In 1968, ten years after the Munich tragedy, Matt's United became the first English team to win the European Cup.

*For his bravery and achievements Matt was knighted by the Queen and became **Sir** Matt Busby.*

He finally retired from the game in 1971 having created two great United sides. Sir Matt won the league title five times, the FA Cup twice and the European Cup once. He became president of the club before dying in 1994, aged 84. Sir Matt Busby will never be forgotten.

SIR MATT BUSBY

But Sir Matt's time was nearly up at Old Trafford and Denis Law, George Best and Bobby Charlton would soon leave too.

Denis was given a free transfer to Manchester City by new manager Tommy Docherty. That decision would come back to haunt Tommy …

Barely a year later, in April 1974, United went into the last game of the season knowing they would be relegated to the Second Division (now the Championship) if they lost.

Their opponents that day were City.

With just a few minutes to play, Denis scored a back-heeler which put his old side down. After so many great years at Old Trafford he could not bring himself to celebrate and instead walked slowly back to the centre circle.

Tommy's team returned to the top flight immediately and went on to win the 1977 FA Cup – beating Liverpool 2–1 to stop them becoming the first English team to win the treble.

But it was not enough to save the Doc from the sack.

By 1981, Ron Atkinson was the man in charge at Old Trafford.

The FA Cup provided United's only taste of glory under Big Ron.

Northern Irish hero Norman Whiteside became the youngest player to score in an FA Cup final when he netted in the replay against Brighton in 1983.

He then scored the winning goal against Everton two years later.

Kevin Moran had earlier become the first player to be sent off in an FA Cup final so United won the '85 Cup with only ten men.

But United were still no closer to winning the league – it was now 20 years since they last lifted the famous trophy – and Big Ron was fired.

RED DEVILS

United became known as the Red Devils after Sir Matt Busby heard it used as the nickname for the red-shirted Salford rugby league side. He thought the 'nasty' devil would make other teams fear United.

By the end of the 1960s, the devil was included on club programmes and scarves before it was finally made part of the club badge in 1970. Now when football fans around the world see a red devil they think of Manchester United.

Alex Ferguson became the new king of Old Trafford.

He already had great players like Bryan Robson and Mark Hughes at the club and would go on and sign stars like Brian McClair, Steve Bruce and Paul Ince.

After three years without a trophy some fans called for Alex to be sacked. But he refused to give up and his first success came in the FA Cup (yes, again!) with a 1–0 replay win over Crystal Palace in 1990.

United were now going places – in fact they went all the way to Rotterdam to play Barcelona in the final of the European Cup Winners' Cup.

Mark Hughes put his team ahead then scored a second from what seemed to be an impossible angle to give United their second European trophy.

It would not be their last …

Alex Ferguson – Fergie to the fans – was now building a new team made up of players like Denis Irwin and Gary Pallister and a great Danish goalkeeper in Peter Schmeichel. A young Welsh boy called Ryan Giggs had also broken into the side.

United were getting closer to the championship.

They should have won it in 1992 but lost out to Leeds. But the long wait was almost over.

United signed Leeds' best player, Eric Cantona, for £1 million. It turned out to be the bargain of the century.

The Elland Road side might as well have handed over the league trophy at the same time!

The French genius scored in four of his first six games and United went on to win the first ever Premier League.

That summer United signed Irish midfielder Roy Keane for a record £3.75million.

Keano helped the Reds win the league again. They then thumped Chelsea 4–0 in the FA Cup final to secure the club's first ever double.

Fergie's team lost the title by just one point to Blackburn Rovers and the FA Cup by a single goal to Everton the following year.

But Fergie did not panic.

The manager, like Matt Busby before him, decided to put his faith in the young players already at the club.

They included David Beckham, Paul Scholes, Nicky Butt and brothers Gary and Phil Neville.

Experts said there was no way you could win anything with kids. And when Newcastle pulled 12 points clear of United by January 1996, it looked as if they were right …

But Alex's spirit and determination rubbed off on the players and they won the title on the last day of the season.

The celebrations did not end there.

A week later Eric Cantona scored a brilliant, late winning goal against Liverpool in the FA Cup final.

It was the first time any team had won the double twice – the 'double double'.

Could it get any better? Oh, yes!

In the first game of the 1996–97 season David Beckham scored against Wimbledon from inside his own **half**!

At the end of another great season Eric Cantona was among the players to hold up the league trophy for the fourth time in five years. He then left fans in tears when he shocked the football world by retiring early from the game.

It took everyone at the club a year to get over Eric leaving, but in true United style they bounced back even stronger. Season 1998–99 was to become the greatest ever in United's history …

Again the race for the title went down to the last day. United led Arsenal by a point and had to beat Tottenham to be champions.

Spurs looked as if they were going to spoil the party when they went 1–0 ahead.

But David Beckham and Andy Cole grabbed a goal each to spark wild celebrations.

The Reds then met old foes Arsenal in the semi-final of the FA Cup. In an amazing game, Roy Keane was sent off, Peter Schmeichel saved a penalty then Ryan Giggs scored one of the best goals of all time to win the tie.

United could now dream of becoming the first English team to win a treble – league, Cup and Champions League.

They made sure they got two trophies out of two when they won the FA Cup 2–0 against Newcastle.

Now it was on to Barcelona for the biggest game in 31 years …

United had already knocked out Inter Milan and Juventus, and now German giants Bayern Munich lay in wait in the Champions League final.

The game started badly and Bayern went 1–0 ahead after just five minutes.

With the clock ticking away it began to look unlikely that Fergie could repeat the feat of Sir Matt.

But Fergie – and United – never give up and they produced one of the most stunning comebacks of all time.

With the game moving into injury time, the ball broke to Teddy Sheringham inside the box and he guided it into the back of the net.

But United would not settle for extra-time and with almost the last kick of the game Ole Gunnar Solskjaer hit the winning goal.

United were champions of Europe again.

SIR ALEX FERGUSON

Alexander Chapman Ferguson was born in Govan, Scotland, on December 31, 1941.

He was manager of East Stirling and St Mirren before working wonders at Aberdeen – making them a better side than Celtic and Rangers and winning the European Cup Winners' Cup.

Premier League
1993, 1994, 1996, 1997, 1999, 2000, 2001, 2003, 2007

FA Cup
1990, 1994, 1996, 1999, 2004

League Cup
1992, 2006

Champions League
1999

European Cup Winners' Cup
1991

He took over at Old Trafford in 1986 and immediately showed who was boss with a tough no-nonsense style.

Under Fergie, United have won nine league championships and five FA Cups.

In 1999, he came the first manager to lead an English team to a treble – league, FA Cup and Champions League. Like Sir Matt before him Fergie was knighted and is now know as Sir Alex.

He is also the only manager ever to win three successive league titles – in 1999, 2000 and 2001.

Sir Alex is now the most successful manager in the history of English football and he hasn't finished yet!

United won the Premiership again in 2000 and then made it three in a row the following year. Arsenal won the double in 2002 but Fergie was determined to get the Red Devils back to the top.

He signed Rio Ferdinand from Leeds United for £30million and the big defender helped United recapture the league title.

United would again lose their grip on the trophy to Arsenal the following year before Chelsea won the Premiership two years in a row after spending hundreds of millions of pounds buying the best players in the world.

But in 2006–07 all the money in the world could not have stopped United.

The Reds – with Cristiano Ronaldo and Wayne Rooney now the stars of the team – showed once again that they were the best in England when they won the title back with three games to spare.

United were champions again!

In a great history Manchester United have won the league title 16 times, the FA Cup a record 11 times, the League Cup twice, the European Cup twice and the European Cup Winners' Cup once.

In Sir Matt Busby and Sir Alex Ferguson they have had two of the best managers the game has ever seen.

And with great players at the club like Wayne Rooney and Cristiano Ronaldo the Red flag will continue to fly high …